Community Services

Careers for Today
Community Services

Marjorie Rittenberg Schulz

Franklin Watts

New York • London • Toronto • Sydney

Developed by: 🔱 **Visual Education Corporation**
Princeton, NJ

Cover Photography: Monkmeyer Press Photo Service, Inc.

Photo Credits: p. 6 Visual Education Archives; p. 9 Michal Heron
/Woodfin Camp & Associates; p. 12 Earl Dotter; p. 14 American
Correctional Association; p. 20 Scott Thode/International Stock
Photography; p. 23 Scott Thode/International Stock Photography; p.
26 Hewlett Packard; p. 29 E.R. Degginger/Bruce Coleman, Inc.; p. 32
Michal Heron/Woodfin Camp & Associates; p. 35 Earl Dotter; p. 38
Michal Heron/Woodfin Camp & Associates; p. 41 Stenograph
Corporation; p. 44 Lee Foster/Bruce Coleman, Inc.; p. 47 Mark
Sherman/Bruce Coleman, Inc.; p. 50 Cameron Davidson/Bruce
Coleman, Inc.; p. 53 United States Navy; p. 56 Earl Dotter; p. 59 John
Zoiner/International Stock Photography; p. 62 Robert Bruschini/
Lower Bucks Family YMCA; p. 67 Robert Bruschini/Lower Bucks
Family YMCA; p. 68 Bill Hubart/Bruce Coleman, Inc.; p. 71
American Association of School Librarians; p. 74 Lew Merrim/
Monkmeyer Press Photo Service, Inc.; p. 77 Spencer Grant/
Monkmeyer Press Photo Service, Inc.; p. 80 Grant LeDuc/
Monkmeyer Press Photo Service, Inc.

Library of Congress Cataloging-in-Publication Data

Schulz, Marjorie Rittenberg.
Community services / Marjorie Rittenberg Schulz.
p.   cm. -- (Careers for today)
Includes bibliographical references (p.   )
Summary: Describes the various careers available in the field of
community services and provides suggestions for students who may be
interested in obtaining such work.
ISBN 0-531-10972-0
1. Human services--Vocational guidance--United States--Juvenile
literature. [1. Human services--Vocational guidance.
2. Vocational guidance.] I. Title. II. Series: Schulz, Marjorie
Rittenberg. Careers for today.
HV10.5.S38 1990
361.'.0023'73--dc20   90-12251 CIP AC

Contents

Introduction

It's February. Ten degrees below zero outside. Zack's apartment feels like ten degrees below zero inside. His heat doesn't seem to be working. Whom will he call?

Mr. and Mrs. Faloba both work at jobs outside the home. Their daughter Susan is three years old and attends Over the Rainbow Preschool from 9:00 A.M. until 12:00 noon each day. So the Falobas need to work out a plan for child care from 12:00 noon until 5:00 P.M. Whom will they call?

For Zack and the Falobas, the answers to these questions are easy. Zack will call the power company to check out his heating system. And the Falobas will call a day-care center for Susan. These are just two of the many community services that people depend on.

About one in every six workers in the United States works in community services. This means nearly 19 million jobs, with new opportunities for workers every day, in government, in public services, in social services, and in private companies that serve the community.

This book can help high school graduates find out about jobs in community services. The jobs in this field are as different as the people who will fill them. So graduates can follow their interests to find jobs that are right for them.

Community Services Today

There is a wide variety of jobs in community services:

Police officer	Paralegal aide
Fire fighter	Court reporter
Crime lab technician	Armed services
Security guard	enlistee
Peace Corps	Electric power
volunteer	worker
Charity fund-raiser	Refuse worker
Child-care worker	Teacher's aide
Elderly-care worker	Immigration officer

Some jobs do not require special training. For jobs that do, many employers will train workers and pay them while they learn on the job.

The future looks bright for high school graduates interested in jobs in community services. As the graph shows, some jobs are growing faster than others. So it is important to look into a job before making a decision.

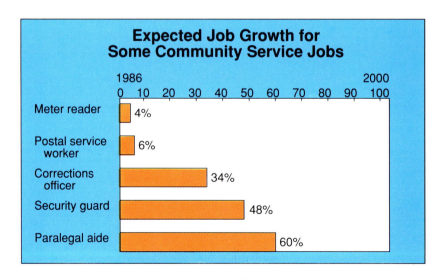

Expected Job Growth for Some Community Service Jobs

Police officers and state troopers are familiar government workers.

Federal, State, and Local Government Services

Federal, state, and local governments provide millions of jobs for people. Look at the numbers:

GOVERNMENT JOBS	
Federal government (civilian)	3 million
Federal government (armed forces)	2 million
State government	4 million
Local government	over 10 million

Seventy-five percent of the jobs in the federal government are office jobs. For many of them, people must pass a civil service examination. The exam guarantees that people are hired on the basis of merit and suitability for the job.

There are excellent opportunities for careers in the armed forces. Recruits get vocational training that can be used both in the military and in civilian life.

9

Federal Wage Systems

Most federal workers are paid under the General Pay Schedule. This has eighteen pay grades that increase according to the responsibilities of the job. A high school graduate with no experience might start at GS-2, or the second level, and move to higher levels as responsibilities increase. Some federal workers are hired under a different system called the Federal Wage System.

As we head toward the year 2000, we will see little overall growth in federal government jobs. But many openings will come from workers retiring or being transferred to other jobs.

State and Local Employment

The number of employees in state and local governments is increasing every year. There are expected to be at least 15 million state and local workers by the year 2000. A big reason for this is the tremendous growth of our cities and suburbs.

Some jobs might be open in the summer, in county courthouses, fire departments, and town recreation centers.

This book will tell you about the following government jobs: corrections officer, police officer, detective, crime lab technician, court reporter, member of the armed services, and fire fighter. Interested high school graduates can contact places like these:

- Town, city, or county government offices
- Governor's office and the offices of state agencies
- Offices of federal agencies or members of Congress

At present, governments are trying to spend less money on community services. Private groups, however, will take over many of these services. These groups will continue to offer satisfying careers to people who care about other people and the way they live.

Public Services

Public services include refuse pickup, gas and electric service, road maintenance, prison control, public library services, legal aid, and work for religious organizations and public-interest groups.

Summer jobs are available for library aides, refuse workers, and construction workers. When full-time workers go on vacation, employers often look to high school graduates to fill in. Part-time jobs may be available to high school students before they have graduated. Sometimes such work can become full-time employment after graduation.

Some jobs—such as legal aide and refuse worker—are expected to grow at a high rate between now and the year 2000. In this book, you can read about the following public service careers: refuse worker, paralegal aide, and electric power service worker.

Interested readers who want more information can write or call:
- Local libraries
- Local government agencies
- Private maintenance, construction, and sanitation contractors
- Public-interest groups

11

Workers in child-care centers provide a caring and loving environment for children.

Social Services

Social services include jobs in child care, care for the elderly, family services, education, and charity fund-raising.

This book tells you about child-care workers. Many new jobs in child care will be available in the coming years.

Care for the elderly, or geriatric care, will be in greater demand as well. People are living longer, and adults with families are often unable to care for elderly parents. So people will look to senior citizens homes and convalescent centers to provide care for the elderly. You can read about geriatric-care workers in this book, too.

You can also read about teacher's aides, who often help out in the classroom. Today, we are becoming more and more concerned with the importance of being able to read. Teacher's aides can help promote the importance of literacy.

12

Private Companies Providing Community Services

Private companies providing community services include security protection firms, some refuse collection companies, public maintenance companies, legal firms, and secretarial services. Over 4 million people in the United States today are employed by private companies that provide services to towns and cities.

Because governments are cutting their budgets, many activities once handled only by govment workers are moving to private companies. For example, certain police duties are being handled by private security firms. Workers in these companies often provide similar services to those in government. While the work is the same, procedures for hiring will differ between government and private jobs.

The future job outlook for security guards is excellent. One reason for the job openings in this area is the increasing number of new stores and industries starting up across the country. This means a greater need for security services to protect these businesses, their jobs, and their employees. This book tells what security workers do.

There will be many jobs coming up for paralegal aides in a variety of businesses. They will be needed in insurance agencies, banks, real estate firms, and other types of companies. You can also read about paralegal aides in this book.

Chapter 1
Corrections Officer, Police Officer, Detective

Law enforcement is an important field in community services. Our daily lives depend on keeping order in our communities and making sure that people are treated fairly. People who break the law must be brought to justice. And citizens in the community must be protected from criminals.

Many different jobs belong to the law enforcement field. This chapter looks at three of them.

Corrections Officer

Education, Training, and Salary   Corrections officers, or prison guards, must have a high school diploma. Applicants take a written exam to test their ability to read and follow directions, as well as a physical exam. A civil service exam and a psychological exam are required in some states. High school courses in communications and government are helpful.

Training takes one to six months and includes courses in correctional methods, defense, and riflery skills.

County corrections officers earn $15,000 to $20,000 per year. State corrections officers earn $17,000 per year and up. Federal corrections officers earn up to $34,000 per year, with benefits including medical insurance, paid vacations, and a retirement plan.

Corrections officers are responsible for the day-to-day safety and security of prisoners. They take prisoners to and from their cells, supervise work and recreational hours, and patrol the buildings. They often must handle prisoner complaints.

Training in the use of weapons, handcuffs, and other restraints is a very important part of the corrections officer's job. Officers must always be alert to be able to act quickly and keep calm in an emergency, such as an attempted escape. They must respect the prisoners and also protect their own safety in a dangerous situation.

Outlook for Jobs   More corrections officers are needed in state prisons than in federal prisons. Young people can apply to any state or county correctional institution. Also, it's a good idea to check with state employment services for current job openings.

After getting experience, corrections officers can move up to the rank of sergeant or lieutenant. This means more responsibility and higher pay.

The outlook through the year 2000 for corrections officers is excellent. New jobs will be opening up as more officers are needed for existing prisons, as older officers retire, and as new prisons are built.

16

Police Officer and Detective

Education, Training, and Salary   Most police departments require candidates to have a high school diploma and to be twenty-one years old. (Some departments allow younger high school graduates to start as trainees or cadets). Height, weight, and eyesight may be factors. A civil service exam may be required, as well as a character and background check.

Classroom training often takes place in a police academy, and lasts three to six months or longer, with further on-the-job training for three to twelve months. Would-be detectives train first as police officers, with detective training ranging from six weeks to several months.

Police officers earn $18,000 and up per year; detectives' salaries range from $17,000 to $30,000 per year. Both jobs receive full benefits.

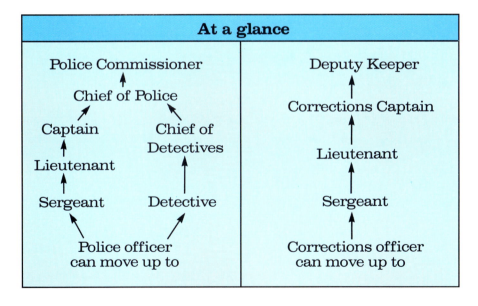

At a glance

Police Commissioner
↑
Chief of Police
↗   ↘
Captain   Chief of
↑   Detectives
Lieutenant   ↑
↑   Detective
Sergeant
↖   ↗
Police officer
can move up to

Deputy Keeper
↑
Corrections Captain
↑
Lieutenant
↑
Sergeant
↑
Corrections officer
can move up to

Job Description   Whether in small towns or large cities, police officers may do one or more of the following:

- Patrol on foot or in squad cars
- Direct traffic and file accident reports
- Work in crime labs or with police records
- Testify at court hearings
- Work in crime prevention
- Educate children about crime

Police work can be very dangerous. Police officers must be able to think and act quickly in emergencies. Since communities need round-the-clock protection, there are police officers on duty at all times. Officers are always on call and must be able to go to work on short notice.

VIOLENT CRIME IN CITIES
(PER 100,000 PEOPLE)

Safest Cities	Violent Crime Rate[a]	Most Dangerous Cities	Violent Crime Rate[a]
1. Grand Forks, ND	53	1. Miami-Hialeah, FL	1,650
2. Bismarck, ND	57	2. New York, NY	1,633
3. Sheboygan, WI	59	3. Los Angeles-Long	1,211
4. Fargo, ND-Moorhead, MN	67	Beach, CA	
5. Rochester, MN	69	4. Flint, MI	1,147
6. St. Cloud, MN	70	5. Baltimore, MD	1,041
7. Nashua, NH	72	6. Chicago, IL	1,037
8. Binghamton, NY	73	7. Baton Rouge, LA	996
9. Eau Claire, WI	74	8. Jacksonville, FL	973
10. Kokomo, IN	78	9. West Palm Beach-Boca Raton-Delray Beach, FL	965
		10. Memphis, TN-AR-MS	948

Source: FBI, *Crime in the United States, 1984, 1985, 1986, 1987, and 1988.*
[a]The violent crime rate is the sum of rates for murder, robbery, and aggravated assault.

Detectives often work behind the scene, examining evidence and putting together clues to solve crimes. Some belong to the local police department; others work on their own as private detectives (for less money, usually, and no benefits). Police detectives often make arrests, with help from uniformed officers.

Private detectives may be hired by lawyers to find out information for trials, by families to find a missing person, or by a company to investigate a crime. They may work as bodyguards, security guards, or store or hotel detectives. Private detectives may not make arrests; they must work with police to bring a suspect into custody.

Outlook for Jobs   The future for police officers and police detectives looks fair. The amount of community funds available plays a crucial role in the number of jobs that will open up. Advancement to senior positions occurs, but may take years. Jobs for private detectives may be more promising, as more companies are hiring detectives to protect their clients or customers.

For more information on corrections officers, police officers, and detectives, write to:

American Correctional Association
4321 Hartwick Road
College Park, MD 20740
(301) 699–7600

Fraternal Order of Police
2100 Gardiner Lane
Louisville, KY 40205
(502) 451–2700

Chapter 2
Security Guard

Security guards are hired to protect people or their property. Security guards work for private businesses such as hotels, restaurants, and stores, or apartment houses. Some work at public buildings, such as government offices or museums.

Education, Training, and Salary

Most employers require candidates to have a high school diploma. Many train guards on the job. Some provide classroom training to teach emergency procedures, alarm systems, and first aid. Civil service exams are required for jobs with the federal government.

Security guards in private companies earn $12,000 to $19,000 per year. Those in the federal government earn up to $16,000 per year.

Job Description

Security guards make sure that buildings are locked, windows and doors are secured, alarms are set, and sprinkler systems are working. They check the identification of people coming into buildings. They also might check the contents of packages.

A guard might work alone or with a guard dog or with several other guards.

In an emergency, a security guard might call the police, paramedics, or fire department for help.

A security guard's job may be a dangerous one. This is especially true if he or she is guarding a building or area that might be subject to burglary. Factories or loading docks that have many deliveries, for instance, can be places that attract thieves. Guards often are armed with a gun for protection and a two-way radio to keep contact with their company or with a main security station. Some guards use closed-circuit televisions or cameras to watch certain areas.

Bonded or *insured* are words used with security guards. Companies that bond and insure security guards look carefully into the person's background. They make sure the person does not have a criminal record, can be relied on, and is a trustworthy person. If so, the person is bonded and may work in security.

Security guards patrol the areas they protect, so they are on their feet for long periods of time. They may work day or night, depending on the buildings they are responsible for. Shifts often have to be scheduled so that there are guards on duty at all hours, seven days a week.

Outlook for Jobs

It is sometimes necessary to start out as a temporary or part-time security guard. This can lead to a full-time job when more experience is gained.

With experience, a security guard can move up to a supervisor job. Security guards who work in government have very good chances to advance.

The job outlook is excellent for security guards for the future. With more and more retail stores and industrial plants under construction, more security will be needed.

Some companies are moving toward electronic security. So some security guards may be replaced by this equipment in the future. However, the equipment must still be maintained by people, so jobs will be available.

Many young people may get seasonal jobs as security guards. Retail places like large department stores hire extra guards during holidays. They also hire extra help at times when they expect more customers, like during large sales. This part-time work gives good experience to young people still in school.

Security officers use closed-circuit televisions to help them monitor many areas at one time.

Talking About the Job

My name is Tim Goodman and I am nineteen years old. I work as a night security guard at Dolman Electronics, a big place on the south side of town.

Rusty, a German shepherd guard dog, works with me here. He is trained to see, hear, and smell people coming. Before he worked here, the company used him at the airport to find illegal drugs. Boy, he tore apart more than a few suitcases in his time!

My job here is to make sure nobody suspicious tries to get inside the Dolman warehouse or offices. If anyone were to come on the grounds, I'd ask them for identification and what their business was.

When Dolman hired me, they trained me on a riflery range with target practice so I could protect myself with a gun if I had to. I've worked here for seven months and haven't used it yet. I hope I never have to, but I'm glad I have it to protect myself just in case.

I work the 11:00 P.M. to 7:00 A.M. shift. So most of the people who work here during the day are gone. The cleaning staff works at night too, so I have to check their schedule every day to see whose shift it is. That way I know who to look for so there won't be any surprises.

It's kind of quiet at night, but I don't mind. I patrol the outside of the building, and then I go inside. I check locks on windows and doors to make sure they are secure. I do a safety check on the fire and burglar alarms to be sure they are working. I get a lot of exercise walking around this place!

I usually read a magazine or the newspaper and have some coffee on my breaks. But I feel like I'm only reading with one eye because I'm always watching and listening.

I like being a security guard because I'm pretty much my own boss. No one is standing over me since I work alone. I know my job and I think I'm pretty good at it.

The security company I work for says I'll be able to work the day shift before too long. That will be really different since there are so many people around here during the day. It will bring a whole different set of challenges, I know. But I think I'll like that, too.

For more information on security guards,
write to:

**American Federation of State, County and
Municipal Employees**
1625 L Street, NW
Washington, DC 20036
(202) 452–4800

International Association of Security Services
P.O. Box 8202
Northfield, IL 60093
(312) 973–7712

**International Security Officers, Police and
Guards**
8519 Fourth Avenue
Brooklyn, NY 11209
(718) 836–3508

Chapter 3
Crime Laboratory Technician

A crime laboratory technician helps solve the mystery of a crime or accident by looking at the evidence left at the scene. Crime lab technicians inspect bullets that have been removed from a body. They examine hair, blood, or cell tissues. They study written messages and letters. They analyze fingerprints, footprints, or tracks left at the scene. They may also be called on to present scientific findings in court.

Crime lab technicians work with the Federal Bureau of Investigation (FBI) to help solve crimes. They also work in larger police or sheriff's departments.

Education, Training, and Salary

A crime lab technician must have a high school diploma. Courses in math, biology, chemistry, and physics are very helpful. Some labs may require college courses in scientific crime detection.

A civil service exam is required for government positions.

Job Description

When a crime or accident occurs, the crime lab technician, detectives, or police officers collect any evidence they think might help them find out what happened. They take careful notes and photographs to "freeze" the scene before objects and bodies are moved. Sometimes they make a floor plan to show the location of things at the scene.

All findings and evidence are given to police investigators. The investigators piece together the findings and build a case.

These are some types of crime lab technicians:

- Polygraph technician—gives lie detector tests
- Ballistics technician—looks at bullets taken from a body
- Fingerprint technician—analyzes fingerprints or other prints or tracks
- Documents technician—analyzes handwriting on forged checks, blackmail notes, or other letters
- Instruments technician—matches marks on a body to the possible weapon
- Chemical and physical analysis technician—looks at evidence such as hair, blood, or skin samples
- Photography technician—takes pictures of the crime scene

Many pieces of equipment are used in the crime lab. A microscope examines a blood or hair sample. Infrared photography looks at papers. An X-ray machine can see bombs inside packages.

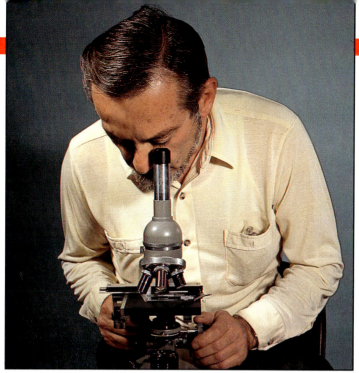
A crime lab technician studies evidence in order to understand a crime.

The work of crime lab technicians involves close study and careful examination of every tiny bit of evidence. Sometimes solving cases depends on the smallest clue.

Outlook for Jobs

Young people interested in a career as a crime lab technician should begin by taking as many science courses as possible. Also important is learning good written communication, since technicians must write very detailed reports of their findings.

A crime lab technician should have a curious mind, enjoy detail, and be able to measure and label a great deal of evidence collected at crime scenes. He or she also must be persistent and stay on a case for long periods of time, if necessary.

Talking About the Job

The Scene: A deserted country road. Deserted except for the victim, lying facedown by the side. There is no evidence of a car accident.

The Solution: ?

This is where I come in. My name is Deborah Witkowski and I am a crime lab technician. I work for a police department in Chicago, along with several other technicians.

Each case is different. For a two-car accident, we collect broken glass, look at skid marks, and check out the direction the cars seem to have been traveling in. We try to recreate the accident to figure out who was at fault and how it might have happened. If someone was badly injured or killed, it becomes even more important to find out the truth.

One case I was involved in was a hit-and-run car accident. A driver was speeding to beat a red light. A teenager didn't see him and stepped off the curb. The driver knocked the boy across the street and sped away. When I arrived on the scene, the police were talking to witnesses, so I went about my job. With plaster casts of the tire tracks and other evidence I found, they were able to trace the car and arrest the driver.

Sometimes it's hard not to think about the people involved. But I have to remember to focus on getting scientific evidence. I have to separate myself from my feelings and do my job.

I'm proud, though, when I help solve a case. By the way, we solved the mystery of the victim on the deserted country road. It appeared as if he had been hit by a car, but we knew it was unlikely since so few cars traveled that road. So we kept searching the scene for clues. About a hundred yards off the road, almost hidden in the thick woods was the answer: a badly damaged motorcycle. Since the victim hadn't been wearing a helmet, it wasn't obvious at first that he had been on a motorcycle. There was a dangerous curve in the road, and he missed it. Case closed.

Beginning crime lab technicians start out working as assistants. As they gain experience, they can move up to an independent position doing one or more types of analysis. Technologists then can move up to become supervisors or project leaders. More responsibility comes with more experience.

The civil service sets ranks for crime lab technicians. Technicians must pass civil service exams to move up to the next rank.

The future is good for young people who want to work as crime lab technicians. Since their work is often the key to solving crimes, good technicians will always be needed.

Most crime lab technicians find a lot of job satisfaction in their work. They know that they can help put criminals behind bars and make their communities safer for people.

For more information on crime lab technicians, write to:

Federal Bureau of Investigation
Ninth Street and Pennsylvania Avenue, NW
Washington, DC 20535
(202) 324–3000

International Order of Chiefs of Police
13 Firstfield Road
Gaithersburg, MD 20878
(301) 948-0922

Chapter 4
Paralegal Aide

People need lawyers to help them settle their legal problems. Lawyers often cannot handle the workload all alone. The people they turn to for help with their cases are paralegal aides.

Aides take on much of the paperwork, research, and preparation that lawyers otherwise would have to do. This frees lawyers to spend more time on giving legal advice and preparing their cases.

Education, Training, and Salary

A high school diploma is required for paralegal aides. Paralegal aides need additional training, too. Hundreds of paralegal training programs are available today. Most take two years to complete. Paralegal aides who work for the federal government must take civil service exams.

Many paralegals start out as secretaries and get valuable experience working in law offices. This step is an excellent way to earn a salary while taking paralegal courses on the side.

Paralegals may start at $13,000 to $16,000 per year. Experienced aides may earn $21,000 and up.

Government paralegals earn about $28,000 per year. Benefits include paid vacations and holidays, medical insurance, and retirement pay.

Job Description

Some paralegal aides work for trial attorneys. These aides are responsible for researching laws and collecting facts to help the lawyers prepare cases for trial. They keep files and organize correspondence such as letters and legal forms.

Other aides work in real estate law or civil law. They may help with home mortgages, contracts, or other documents. They might deal with companies and corporations who need agreements drawn up for employees.

Some paralegals work for the government. They may be involved with health and safety practices and with helping to draft laws to protect workers. They work with legal documents and make sure laws are fair to the rights of citizens.

Community service is an important area for paralegal aides, who might help the poor or the elderly. Paralegals may file forms for clients who otherwise would not know their rights.

Some paralegal aides work in groups involved with the environment or consumer protection. A group of people may not want a power plant built in their town because of the pollution it would cause. So a paralegal aide might help them fight the construction of the power plant by telling them what legal steps they can take.

Aides also work for accounting firms and banks. They might assist accountants and bankers in drawing up legal papers and researching laws that apply to their field.

Much of a paralegal's work is done in law libraries. So someone interested in the profession should like reading, researching in books, and organizing information.

34

A lawyer works closely with paralegal aides. They are told the details of a case before they begin their research.

A paralegal might be asked to check facts and find cases that are similar to the one the lawyer is working on. The paralegal may need to find a *precedent,* or an instance of the same type of situation.

Paralegals need good writing skills. Helping to prepare legal briefs and assemble information for court cases takes organizational skills and the ability to communicate clearly. Much of the paralegal's work is done on computers today.

Paralegals can specialize in one area of law if they choose. They may settle on a specialty such as environmental law or real estate law.

Paralegals may be called upon to work overtime.

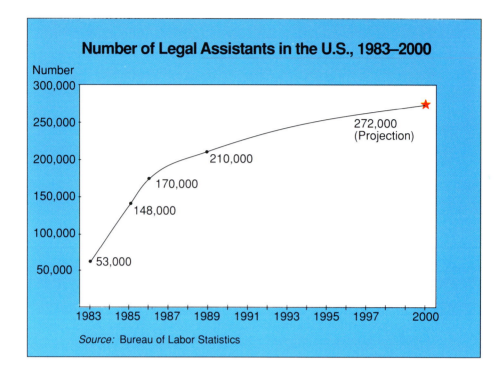

Number of Legal Assistants in the U.S., 1983–2000

Number

300,000

250,000

200,000

150,000

100,000

50,000

53,000

148,000

170,000

210,000

272,000
(Projection)

1983 1985 1987 1989 1991 1993 1995 1997 2000

Source: Bureau of Labor Statistics

Outlook for Jobs

People interested in becoming paralegal aides should apply directly to lawyers' offices or to government offices.

Young people start out as assistants and move up to become paralegal aides. They may then be appointed as supervisors to oversee other aides. Moving from a small law office to a larger law firm can help paralegals advance in their careers.

The future looks excellent for paralegal aides. By 2000, the number of paralegals is expected to grow to almost 300,000. This will be the fastest growing profession in the coming years. In the next twenty years, there may even be more legal assistants than lawyers!

For more information on paralegals, write to:

American Bar Association
750 N. Lake Shore Drive
Chicago, IL 60611

National Association of Legal Assistants, Inc.
1601 S. Main Street
Tulsa, OK 74119–4452
(918) 587–6828

National Federation of Paralegal Associations
P.O. Box 40158
Overland Park, KS 66204

National Paralegal Association
P.O. Box 629
60 E. State Street
Doylestown, PA 18901

Chapter 5
Shorthand or Court Reporter

During a court trial or a business proceeding, every word that is said is important to the final decision made by a judge or a jury. An official record of a trial or proceeding helps decide the final outcome.

The workers who take down everything that is said are shorthand reporters or court reporters. They make a permanent record by using their training and skills.

Education, Training, and Salary

A high school diploma is required to become a shorthand or court reporter.

Shorthand or other stenographic and typing skills are necessary. Shorthand reporters must be able to take about 160 words of dictation a minute. Civil service exams are required for jobs in state or federal agencies and courts.

Most secretarial or business schools provide training for these jobs. Courses include shorthand, typing, transcribing, medical terminology, legal phrases, Latin words and phrases, English, editing, business law, court procedure, and economics.

Most beginning shorthand or court reporters earn about $17,000 to $19,000 a year. Reporters with many years' experience can earn as much as

$50,000 a year. Benefits include medical insurance and retirement plans.

Free-lance court reporters, who are in business for themselves, may earn more than salaried reporters. But free-lancers do not receive benefits.

Job Description

Shorthand reporters write in shorthand, using symbols or abbreviations instead of writing out whole words. By doing this, they can record a lot of information very quickly.

Some shorthand reporters use stenotype machines. This machine has twenty-one keys, and the typed record comes out on a pad or roll of paper. After the shorthand reporters take all their notes, they transcribe it, or write it out in complete reports so that others can read it.

About one-half of all shorthand reporters are court reporters. They work in courts, from local traffic courts all the way up to the U.S. Supreme Court. In smaller towns, reporters might work in many different courts, going from one to another where they are needed. In large areas, they probably will be assigned to one court.

Speed and accuracy are very important in recording information. A missed word or incorrect statement may affect a jury's opinion about a witness.

Sometimes court reporters are asked to read aloud what they have recorded. This often happens when something needs to be repeated or removed from the record.

The government includes similar jobs. Hearing reporters perform this job in agencies. A hearing is like a trial, where lawyers represent

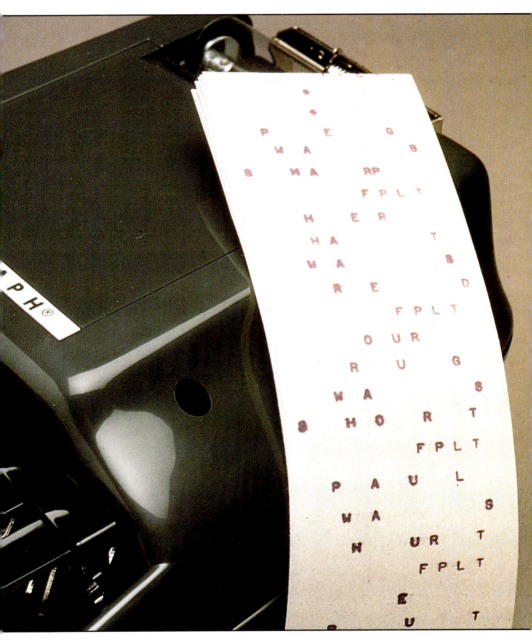

Shorthand reporters record every word spoken during a
trial with the aid of a stenotype machine.

people. Legislative reporters record proceedings in the Senate or the House of Representatives.

Some companies hire out general or free-lance reporters. They usually work at temporary jobs when they are needed for short times.

Outlook for Jobs

Shorthand and court reporters move up by taking and passing civil service exams at each level. They can advance by transferring from smaller state and federal agencies to federal courts.

The outlook is very good for shorthand and court reporters through the year 2000. Government and business will continue to grow, with more trials, conferences, and meetings to record. So there will always be a need for skilled reporters in the future. In fact, right now there is a shortage of shorthand reporters in most areas of the United States.

The first shorthand report of a trial was made by John Llywellin, Clerk of the Council, who was instructed by Lord Baltimore to record the proceedings held in the Provincial Court, St. Johns, Maryland, on November 15, 1681. The Justices Tailoor, Stevens, and Diggens found Josias Fendall guilty of mutiny on March 26, 1681, and sentenced him to pay "40,000 pounds of Tobacco for a fine, Be kept in safe custody at [his] own proper costes and charges until [he] shall have paid the same and after the same is paid to be for ever banished out of this Province." (Maryland Archives, Vol. 5)

Source: Joseph Nathan Kane, Famous First Facts, 4th ed. New York: H. W. Wilson, p. 81.

For more information on shorthand and court reporters, write to:

National Shorthand Reporters Association

118 Park Street
Vienna, VA 22180
(703) 281–4677

Chapter 6
Refuse Worker

Disposal of waste materials is a service we cannot live without. In fact, our country is becoming so crowded that we must start thinking more about the ways we dispose of waste.

Education, Training, and Salary

Private companies and cities that hire refuse workers prefer workers with a high school or a vocational school education. Beginning workers are trained on the job. They work alongside experienced workers and learn by watching and doing. For government jobs, refuse workers must take civil service exams or other tests.

Wages for refuse workers depend on the specific job and on the area of the country in which they work. Starting salaries for young people begin at $15,000. Experienced truck drivers may earn $26,000 or more a year.

Workers in larger cities tend to earn more than those in smaller towns. Most refuse workers join labor unions. Workers enjoy paid holidays and vacations, medical insurance, workers' compensation, and retirement plans.

Job Description

Refuse workers collect garbage and other waste and deliver it to disposal sites. They lift large containers, drive trucks, operate heavy equipment, and often go on their routes in bitter cold, heavy rain, or very hot weather.

Collectors usually work in crews that service neighborhoods in towns and cities.

Two kinds of refuse workers work at disposal areas. Landfill operators are responsible for dumping waste where it will be buried. They operate heavy equipment to deposit garbage and to cover it with dirt. The other kind of worker—incinerator operators—are responsible for burning waste materials. They use coal or other fuel to light large furnaces. After the trash is burned, they remove ashes from the furnaces.

Outlook for Jobs

Young people usually start out as laborers. This may be on a truck route, at an incinerator plant, or at a landfill.

To advance to a higher job, government workers take civil service exams. Workers for private refuse companies may become supervisors, drivers, and incinerator or landfill operators.

The outlook for the future for jobs in refuse collection, disposal, and recycling is fair.

Jobs open up for new refuse workers when older employees retire or move on to other jobs. The push toward recycling in more cities and towns across the country may mean more jobs for refuse workers. Some states are passing strict new laws for recycling. One law states that more recyclable paper be used in newspaper printing. Another limits the amount of unrecyclable material that can be thrown away.

46

Landfill operators use large earth-moving machines to transport and bury refuse.

Recycling for the Future

Today we must start thinking more about our environment. We are making more and more trash and running out of places to put it. Trash can hurt the environment and our health. When waste is burned, it pollutes the air we breathe. Open garbage dumps provide breeding places for rats and flies, which spread disease. And dumping trash into lakes and rivers pollutes our water supply.

Ever wonder how much garbage we make each year in this country? The amount of trash from homes, businesses, and institutions has more than doubled in thirty years:

1960	79 million tons
1978	140 million tons
1990	178 million tons (est.)

Recycling, or reusing trash, is becoming more common. Many communities are starting recycling programs. The most commonly recycled materials are paper, metals, plastics, and glass. Careful separation of these valuable materials from trash is important.

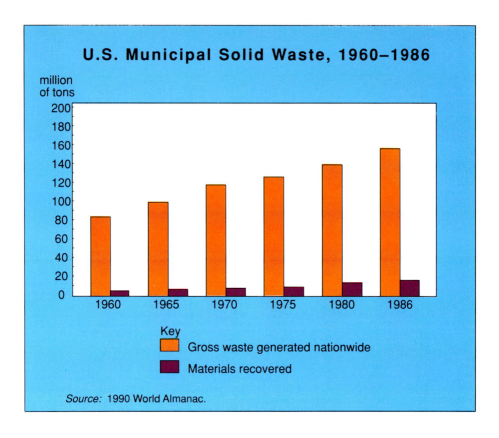

U.S. Municipal Solid Waste, 1960–1986

million of tons

Key
- Gross waste generated nationwide
- Materials recovered

Source: 1990 World Almanac.

Trash can be recycled in two ways. The first is by machine separation at recycling plants. In such a plant, the refuse is shredded, dried, and burned by special machines. Much of the waste is turned into ash, which gets blown away by strong blasts of air. The large pieces left over are separated into glass, aluminum, and other metals. The glass must be sorted into colored and noncolored groups. These recyclable materials are then melted down and reshaped for reuse.

As an added benefit, the energy given off when the waste is burned may be used for heating and power.

The second way to recycle begins at home. It is called separation at the source of disposal. In some communities, people are required by law to sort aluminum cans, glass bottles, newspapers, and waste paper from their other trash. In other places, recycling centers collect empty cans and bottles. Separation at the source saves time and money for recycling centers.

Even when people separate their own trash, refuse workers are needed to collect the objects and take them to a recycling plant. Many cities give residents large containers to collect materials for recycling. Residents are usually charged a one-time fee for the containers. In most cities, they must pay several extra dollars a month for the recycling pickup.

For more information on refuse workers, write to:

American Federation of State, County, and Municipal Employees
1625 L Street, NW
Washington, DC 20036
(202) 452–4800

International Brotherhood of Teamsters, Chauffeurs, Warehousemen, and Helpers of America
25 Louisiana Avenue, NW
Washington, DC 20001
(202) 624–6800

Interested people may also apply at public refuse companies run by their town or city and at private refuse and collection companies.

Chapter 7
Armed Services Career

The armed services include the Army, Navy, Air Force, Marines, and Coast Guard. More than two million men and women serve in the armed services today. Military service is voluntary today, but a draft that requires service of people of a certain age could be set up in an emergency. The armed services offer excellent education and training programs. Thus the military is an attractive career for many young people today.

Education, Training, Salary

Enlistees (persons who join the services) must be seventeen years old and be able to read and write English. Persons joining the Air Force and Marines must have a high school diploma. Enlistments are for three or more years of active duty. Enlistments can also be for six years of reserve duty, four months of which must be on active duty.

Aptitude tests are given before enlistment. Future enlistees may enter any field—or specific training program—for which they qualify and places are open. Persons failing to qualify may reconsider enlisting.

Salaries are paid according to length of service, type of job, and performance level. The average salary for all personnel is $16,500. It is often lower than that paid for comparable civilian jobs. However, military benefits may include free meals and living quarters on bases or off-base living allowances. Medical care, uniforms, vacation, inexpensive life insurance, and retirement pay are also included.

Job Description

The purpose of the military is to train professional fighting personnel and officers to defend their country. It requires having a sense of duty and the willingness to obey orders without question and to accept discipline. Military life involves working and often living together with others. Training requires physical stamina, and combat calls for courage.

Every enlistee must go through basic training, which involves both physical training and classroom study. Following basic training, enlistees are tested and interviewed for placement with suitable jobs or further training. Permanent duty is then assigned. Duty may be anywhere in the world.

Only a small proportion of military personnel are combat ready. Most members of the military work in military bases at noncombat jobs that any civilian might perform. Bases need police and fire protection, as well as medical, clerical, and dietary personnel. They need experts in communications as well as technical, budgetary, supply, maintenance, and transportation advisers. Training for these jobs may result in permanent careers, either in the military or in civilian life after retiring from the military.

The list shows some of the nonmilitary careers for which members of the armed services receive training:

Bookkeeper	Nurse
Bus driver	Paralegal
Carpenter	Physical therapy
Chauffeur	specialist
Clerk	Plumber
Computer specialist	Police officer
Cook	Postal clerk
Corrections officer	Power plant worker
Court reporter	Radio operator
Dental assistant	Sports instructor
Electronics technician	Statistician
Fire fighter	Stenographer
Lab technician	Switchboard operator
Machinist	Truck driver
Maintenance worker	Waiter
Mechanic	X-ray technician

Enlistees often receive training in special areas such as computers.

Outlook for Jobs

Advancement is always available in the armed services. Hard work and leadership ability is rewarded by opportunities for additional training and higher rank. Some fields in the military may become filled. But since the military offers more careers than any other employer, the enlistee will always have many choices.

The future outlook for a military career is good. Congress reviews military pay every year, and it is highly competitive, with its many benefits, to many civilian jobs. In addition, special pay is available for hazardous jobs, such as handling explosives or serving on a submarine.

The armed services offer good career possibilities for women as well as men. Except that they may not serve in combat, women are treated equally with men.

Women in the Military

In August of 1989, a young woman made military history. Kristin M. Baker became the first woman ever to serve the U.S. Military Academy as brigade commander and first captain of the Corps of Cadets. She is the highest-ranking cadet at West Point.

Baker said she was chosen for her abilities by an army that doesn't discriminate. Many women who have chosen careers in the military would agree. Today, women make up 11 percent of the military's 283,000 members. According to the Defense Department, 24,000 positions have been opened to women in the past two years. Congress is increasing pressure on the military to allow women to fight alongside men in battle. If such a law is passed, women will find even greater opportunity for advancement to the highest command positions.

School guidance offices and state employment offices have information about the armed forces.

For more information on the armed forces, write to:

United States Air Force Recruiting Office
1101 Pennsylvania Avenue, NW
Washington, DC 20004
(202) 272–1481

United States Army Recruiting Office
5700 Georgia Avenue, NW
Washington, DC 20011
(202) 282–2512

United States Coast Guard Recruiting Office
312 South Washington Street
Alexandria, VA 22314
(703) 683–7700

United States Marine Corps Recruiting Office
5700 Georgia Avenue, NW
Washington, DC 20011
(202) 282–2540

United States Navy Recruiting Office
5700 Georgia Avenue, NW
Washington, DC 20011
(202) 282–2533

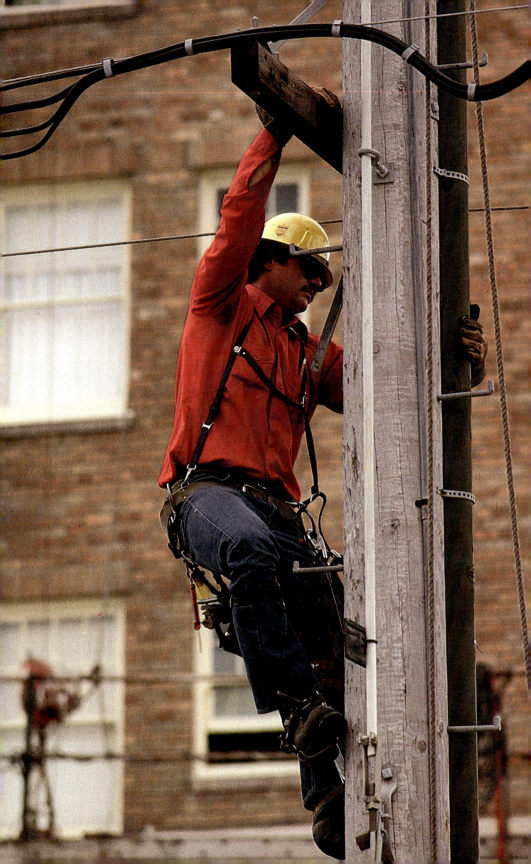

Chapter 8
Electric Power Worker

Since electricity is an important source of power to our homes, industries, and communities, power workers are essential to our lives.

Education, Training, and Salary

Most power service companies prefer to hire high school graduates. Basic knowledge of electricity is essential. High school or vocational courses in shop and electrical work are helpful.

Most electrical power service and transmission workers are trained on the job by more experienced workers. Classroom instruction may also be given in basic electricity, safety, and reading blueprints. Workers who are employed by companies owned by towns or cities may have to pass civil service exams.

Starting jobs for electric meter installers, repairers, and testers usually are from $17,000 to $20,000 per year. District representatives often earn from $22,000 to $26,000 per year. Pay for transmission workers varies, but starts at about $22,000 per year for ground helpers. Line installers and splicers earn more than $500 per week, and experienced workers earn more than $27,000 per year. Benefits may include medical and accident insurance, as well as paid vacations. Workers belonging to unions receive extra benefits, such as retirement pay.

Job Description

Electric power companies use many different kinds of workers. Some work in the offices. Customer service representatives deal with customers on the phone and in person. They answer questions, hear complaints, and discuss electric bills. Service representatives sometimes have to deal with unhappy customers. This is why patience and a cool head are necessary for the customer service worker.

Many electric power workers work outdoors on the power lines and power sources themselves. They normally wear company uniforms to identify themselves.

Load dispatchers say how much electricity should be produced and where it should go. They also arrange for the repair of downed lines.

Substation operators work in small regional stations. They act on the load dispatcher's orders to increase or decrease the amount of electricity for their area.

Line installers put up the power lines that conduct electricity from the power plant to the area where it will be used. They are assisted by ground helpers.

Troubleshooters are line workers who fix transmission lines that aren't working properly. They must have special training in order to work safely with energized lines. They answer emergency calls at all hours and in all kinds of weather so that power can be restored.

Cable splicers inspect and repair connections between cables. They may work on cables strung from power poles or on underground cables.

Some workers read, test, or repair the meters that show how much power is used at a given home or business.

Some smaller electric companies in areas that may not service many houses or businesses have district representatives. They do customer service work and might also perform electrical work. They may check meters and do minor repairs. A trained electric power worker, such as a troubleshooter or cable splicer, would be sent out if big problems occurred or major repairs were needed.

Customer service representatives need to be patient and courteous when working with the public.

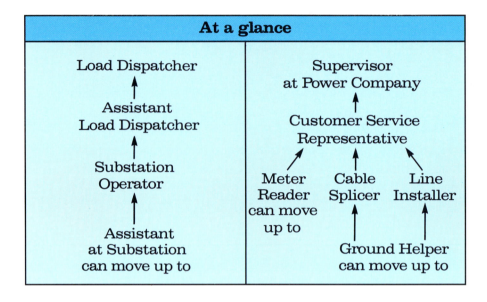

At a glance	
Load Dispatcher ↑ Assistant Load Dispatcher ↑ Substation Operator ↑ Assistant at Substation can move up to	Supervisor at Power Company ↑ Customer Service Representative ↖ ↑ ↖ Meter Cable Line Reader Splicer Installer can move up to ↑ ↑ Ground Helper can move up to

Outlook for Jobs

Electric power workers may move up to more responsibility with higher pay. Ground helpers with experience may move up to become cable splicers or line installers. It usually takes about four years of experience to become a skilled line worker.

Assistants at substations may become substation operators after three to seven years. And substation operators with seven to ten years of experience may become load dispatchers.

Meter readers might take courses in personnel relations or learn more about electrical power. They could then advance to a job in customer service or become a supervisor.

Service representatives also may move up to a position as supervisor. Meter repairers and testers may advance by moving up to larger companies that use more complicated equipment.

60

The number of openings for most electric power jobs should increase, but only slightly. While people are using more electricity than ever, some jobs will be replaced by computers and other automated machines.

Meter readers are an example of this trend toward fewer jobs due to the spread of automation. The need for meter readers will probably decrease in the future. More and more meters will probably be read automatically over telephone lines.

To find a job as an electric power worker, interested young people should contact electric companies. They might also check with high school placement offices and technical schools in their area.

For more information on jobs in electrical power service, write to:

Edison Electric Institute
1111 Nineteenth Street, NW
Washington, D.C. 20036
(202) 778–6400

International Brotherhood of Electrical Workers
1125 Fifteenth Street, NW
Washington, D.C. 20005
(202) 833–7000

Utility Workers Union of America
815 Sixteenth Street, NW
Washington, D.C. 20006
(202) 347–8105

Chapter 9
Child-Care Aide and Geriatric Aide

Child-Care Aide

Child-care aides work with preschoolers. Infants and toddlers need a great deal of positive attention and require much patience. Aides help surround children with a happy and caring atmosphere.

Education, Training, and Salary

Child-care workers need a high school education. They will get on-the-job training from experienced workers. Home economics classes are also helpful.

Many child-care workers enroll in formal programs that include courses in education, nutrition, home economics, and psychology. Many two-year colleges have programs that lead to an associate degree in preschool or early-childhood education.

Salaries vary depending on the area of the country and experience. Child-care aides can earn $8,000 to $12,000 per year. Benefits, including medical insurance, paid holidays and vacations, and retirement pay, are almost always offered.

State-run child-care centers charge parents less than privately owned centers. This may mean lower pay for workers at these centers.

Job Description

Directors of child-care centers provide aides with the games, reading materials, and other activities that are right for certain ages.

It is important for aides to stimulate children's imagination, help them learn physical skills, and encourage them to communicate their thoughts and feelings to others so they can be understood.

Child-care aides are often in charge of making healthful snacks and meals for children. Some children are at centers for eight or more hours, so they may eat all their meals at the center. Aides learn that good nutrition is important to physical and mental growth.

Outlook for Jobs

The outlook as we near the year 2000 is very good for child-care jobs. Some of the reasons for the increased need for child-care workers are:

- More parents are working outside the home.
- Child care is no longer restricted to neighbors, relatives, or churches.
- New child-care centers are opening up at private companies for employees' children.
- Child-care centers are open longer hours.

Geriatric Aide

Education, Training, and Salary   Geriatric aides usually need a high school diploma. They should be trained in CPR, or cardio-pulmonary resuscitation, and in first aid. Other training is on the job.

Geriatric workers earn about $10,000 to $14,000 a year. This may differ from one area of the country to another. Benefits include medical insurance, paid holidays and vacations, and retirement pay.

Talking About the Job

As I stand here in the child-care center, I have three tiny people hanging on to my arms. When they say it takes strength to deal with children, they're not kidding!

I'm Michelle Ito and I am a child-care aide in a large center. I love my job. I have always liked little kids, from the time I started baby-sitting when I was twelve years old. I like to get down on the floor and play games and do exercises to music. And I enjoy listening to their funny made-up stories about everything from spacemen to circus bears.

Some little ones are dropped off at 6:00 A.M., when their parents go to work. Sometimes they are half-asleep, so I either hold them for a while or lay them down to rest. Often the children stay until 5:00 or 6:00 P.M., so they have a pretty long day here.

As you can probably imagine, not all the children *want* to be dropped off here. It's not so much coming here that bothers them. They don't want their parents to leave. It's especially hard for some of the two- and three-year-olds.

We have to calm them and try to take away their fears. We get them interested in a toy or a cracker—anything that will take their mind off their parents. After they've been here a few weeks they get used to us, and they make friends. Then it starts to seem like a second home to them.

I know my job is an important one. The parents tell me how much they appreciate knowing their children are in safe hands each day. And I know this is where I want to be. Especially when I hear a little voice saying, "I love you, Michelle."

Job Description

Geriatric aides care for elderly people in retirement or nursing homes, recreation centers, or private homes.

Some aides help feed, dress, and bathe people. Others lead exercise classes, arts and crafts or music classes, or other recreational programs. And other aides assist medical staff in caring for mentally or physically ill people.

Geriatric aides should enjoy working with elderly people on a daily basis. The job may be stressful and requires sensitivity. Crises often occur. It is helpful to be able to think clearly and use good judgment in an emergency.

Working hours depend on the type of people aides will care for. In nursing homes, residents need care around the clock, so aides may work in shifts.

Outlook for Jobs

The future looks very good for geriatric aides. The elderly population is growing as people live longer. And many children of elderly are becoming elderly themselves and need help in caring for their parents. They are fortunate in being able to turn to elderly-care facilities and qualified workers for help.

Interested young people can apply to private child-care centers in their area. Or they can ask at their state department of education for names of state-run agencies.

Those interested in geriatric care might apply at nursing homes and other centers for the elderly. They also can check with social service agencies in their area.

66

A child-care worker helps preschoolers with their lunches.

For more information on child-care or geriatric-care workers, write to:

National Association for Child Care Management
1255 Twenty-third Street, NW
Washington, DC 20037
(202) 659-5955

National Association for the Education of Young Children
1834 Connecticut Avenue, NW
Washington, DC 20009
(202) 232–8777

National Geriatrics Society
212 West Wisconsin Avenue
Milwaukee, WI 53203
(414) 272–4130

Chapter 10
Teacher's Aide

Working with students and helping them in the classroom can be a very rewarding career for young people. Teacher's aides are valuable helpers in many schools. Their assistance allows teachers to have more time for the students.

Education, Training, and Salary

A high school diploma is usually required for teacher's aides. The education requirement may depend on the grade level with which the aide will be working. An aide may choose to take a teaching aide course in a community college.

Initial training to become a teacher's aide may vary from school to school. Many schools offer one- or two-week training sessions to help the aide become familiar with their system. Much of the training comes on the job, as aides work with students.

Teacher's aides average about $6.00 per hour, with more for instructional aides. With more experience, aides may earn up to $16,000 a year. With more education, responsibilities and salary increase. Benefits vary according to school district.

Job Description

One type of aide is the noninstructional aide. They generally assist the teacher and do many cleanup and organizing chores in the classroom. They might be in charge of keeping the room in order—wiping down blackboards or arranging desks and tables.

An aide might help out by keeping track of classroom supplies and ordering them if needed. Aides may take attendance, keep student records up to date, or designing and preparing bulletin boards in the classrooms and hallways may be part of a teacher's aide job.

Some teacher's aides help out in the school office. They do typing, filing, and copying. When the school secretary takes a lunch or coffee break, the aide fills in until the secretary returns.

Aides may be needed in the school library or resource center to check out books or send out overdue notices to students. Aides also shelve books and make sure all magazines and other materials are in the correct places.

Teacher's aides sometimes set up audiovisual equipment in the classrooms. They might be responsible for equipment such as closed-circuit televisions, slide projectors, videocassette recorders, or tape players.

Aides who help teach are called instructional aides. Those who know how might play a musical instrument during music class. Those who can draw may help with art instruction. In addition, instructional aides may work with students who need help with daily assignments. Teachers often give aides test answers and have them check test papers against the answers.

This teacher's aide is working in the school library putting together a library display.

Teacher's aides can work at any grade level in public or private schools. Most often, aides are needed to help out with younger students.

Aides usually work from September through June, the regular school year. Some aides help out during summer school. They may assist students or help out organizing classrooms.

Aides should like working with young students. They must be able to follow instructions from teachers and administrators. And they should be able to interact well with parents.

Outlook for Jobs

Teacher's aides can begin helping out in schools right after graduation from high school. While they work, aides can take helpful courses at nearby community colleges in education, psychology, and English, for example. The more young people learn, the better teacher's aides they will be.

71

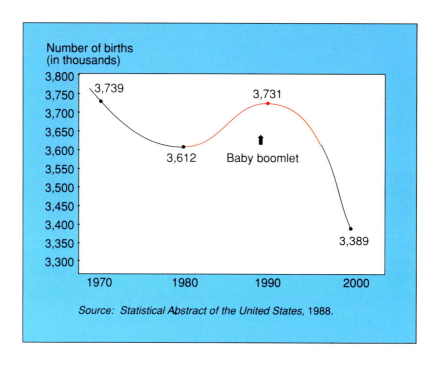

Number of births (in thousands)

3,739

3,731

3,612

Baby boomlet

3,389

1970   1980   1990   2000

Source: *Statistical Abstract of the United States,* 1988.

Outlook for Jobs

Demand for teachers and teacher's aides depends on several things:

- School enrollments—because of an expected baby boomlet in the 1990s, elementary school enrollment is also expected to rise (see the graph above).
- The country's economy—if the economy is good, more government funds may be used to hire aides.
- School budget—if there are enough funds in the school budget, teacher's aides may be hired.

72

- Class size—teachers need more help with larger classes.
- Turnover rate—teacher's aides usually stay in jobs for short periods of time, so openings often occur.

As we head toward 2000, openings for teacher's aides are expected to increase as the school population increases.

For more information on teacher's aides, write to:

American Federation of Teachers
555 New Jersey Avenue, NW
Washington, DC 20001
(202) 879-4400

National Education Association
1201 Sixteenth Street, NW
Washington, DC 20036
(202) 833-4000

People interested in becoming teacher's aides should also check at local schools for openings.

Chapter 11
Fire Fighter

Protecting people, their belongings, and their homes is a valuable service provided by the brave men and women in fire fighting. Fire fighters put their lives on the line.

Education, Training, and Salary

There are no education requirements to become a fire fighter, but a high school education gives young people aged eighteen or older a better chance at passing the civil service exam required. Since the job is very demanding, future fire fighters are tested to make sure that they are physically able to perform the job.

In some fire companies young people train for a few weeks. In others, they work side-by-side with an experienced fire fighter in an apprenticeship program.

Many community colleges offer courses in fire science and fire engineering. These may be necessary to be promoted to upper levels.

Beginning fire fighters earn about $10,000 to $14,000 a year. This varies depending on experience and location. Fire fighters with experience can earn $28,000 a year. Fire chiefs can earn $37,000 a year.

Fire fighters get good benefits such as vacations, medical insurance, sick days, and retirement pay.

Job Description

Fire fighters work at many different jobs within a fire company. They drive the fire trucks, operate the pumps and connect the hoses, guide the ladder carriers, and fight the blazes.

To get into burning buildings, fire fighters use axes to break down walls and enter through windows. They must figure out the safest, fastest ways to get people out of burning buildings.

Fire fighters are trained in first aid to help injured people. They often work on rescue squads, which speed to fires in well-equipped vans. These fire fighters are also called to help with injuries and accidents or to give first aid to people who have suffered heart attacks. They assist the victims until ambulances and paramedics arrive on the scene.

Fire prevention is a big part of the fire company's responsibility. Fire inspectors check out buildings to make sure that fire alarms and sprinkler systems are in working order and escape routes are marked. Prevention is the first defense against fire.

Fire fighters often go into the schools and talk to students about the importance of fire prevention in their homes. They might ask them to map out an escape route using their home's floor plan. A good escape plan can save lives in an emergency.

Fire fighters may work for the town or city government or for private companies. Some fire fighters give their time as volunteer fire fighters and have other regular jobs.

Experts called fire science specialists often work for insurance agencies. They investigate insurance claims from people who have had losses due to fire. They help the insurance agency decide how much money to pay these people.

Fire insurance specialists also inspect public and private buildings to make sure they are as safe as possible and help plan for emergencies.

Fire fighters must wear special gear to protect themselves from flames, heat, and smoke.

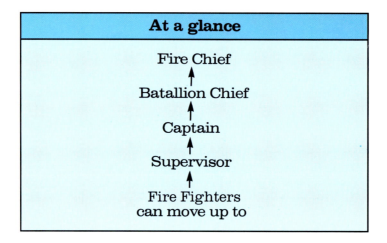

At a glance

Fire Chief
↑
Batallion Chief
↑
Captain
↑
Supervisor
↑
Fire Fighters
can move up to

Fire fighters can move up through the ranks within their departments. They can be promoted if they pass civil service exams and are recommended by their supervisors.

To become fire fighters, young people must be willing to work under dangerous conditions. They must be physically strong and able to act quickly and effectively in emergencies. Often their lives are at risk.

Fire fighters work in shifts during the day or night. Some live at the fire station for certain days. Fire fighters must be able to follow orders and work as part of a team. It is important to keep sharpening fire-fighting skills.

Outlook for Jobs

Today, there are over 300,000 fire fighters in the United States. The future looks fair for those planning to become fire fighters. There is much competition for jobs in larger cities. Openings occur as cities grow and new departments are formed or old departments become larger.

For more information on fire fighters, write to:

National Fire Protection Association
Batterymarch Park
Quincy, MA 02269
(617) 770–3000

International Association of Fire Fighters
1750 New York Avenue, NW
Washington, DC 20006
(202) 737–8484

Chapter 12
Getting the Job: Tips for the Reader

Starting Out

Whatever job you decide to go after, you want to do it to the best of your ability. And you can do this only if you have picked a job you enjoy and feel comfortable with. Be honest with yourself and begin your job search by knowing your talents and interests.

Rate Your Strengths

Write down on a piece of paper a few lines about yourself: what you like, what you dislike, what your favorite subject at school is, what your least favorite subject is, what bores you, what excites you.

Make a chart and list any jobs you have ever had. Include your supervisors' names, your work addresses, and the dates of employment. Now make a list of your hobbies or interests. Also list the schools you have attended and your extracurricular activities. This list would include clubs or teams you belong to. If you have done any volunteer work, be sure to list it. Finally, add to your list the names of any awards or prizes you have won.

List Your Job Possibilities

List all the jobs in this book that sound interesting. Look at each job and see if you qualify. If a job you like requires extra training, write that down. Also check the publications in the back of this book and note the titles of any books or other materials that will tell you more about the jobs you like.

Look at your job list and your strengths list. See where they match up, and put a star by those jobs that would use your strengths.

Consult Counselors

Talk to a guidance counselor at your school about jobs that are open in your field of interest. Your state or local employment service can also help you.

Looking for Work

When you have settled on the jobs you would like, start looking for openings. Apply for as many jobs as you can—the more you apply for, the better your chance of finding one.

Research   Find out everything you can about jobs you are applying for. The more information you have about jobs, employers, and employers' needs, the more impressive you will be in your interview.

Ads   There are two types of newspaper classified ads: *help wanted* and *situation wanted.* A help wanted ad is placed by an employer looking for a worker to fill a specific job. It tells you the job, requirements, salary, company, and whom to contact. Or it is a blind ad, one that just has a post office box number. Answer the ad by letter or by phone, as directed in the ad. Follow up within two weeks with another phone call or letter if you have not heard from the employer.

A person looking for work can place a *situation wanted* ad. This ad tells the kind of work the person is looking for, why he or she qualifies, and when he or she could start working.

Networking Networking is letting everyone know what jobs you're looking for. Talk to people in your field of interest, friends, or relatives who might be able to help. Some good leads on jobs can be found this way. Follow up on what you learn with a phone call or letter.

Employment Services Check with the high school's or vocational school's placement service for job openings. State and local employment services often have job listings.

Classified Ads Help Wanted

PARALEGAL AIDE Small office seeks h.s. grad with some knowledge legal language. Non-smokers only. Will train. $14,500. Excel. bnfts. Write P. Bellows, Schiff, Jordan, and Neely, 448 Main Street, Decatur.

WE NEED PROTECTION — Wanted: Exp. p.t. security guard nights 10-2 A.M. Must have own car. Fill out application in person, 1300 W. Wisconson Ave., Skokie.

Attention, Police Officers: Earn money in your spare time as private detectives. Matrimonial, missing persons work. Send resume, refs. and sal. req. to Undercover Investigations, P.O. Box 1212, Margate.

Westmont Fire Department — needs p/t fire fighters with 3 years exp. Immed. hire. Good benefits. Apply at Westmont Fire Station daily, or call 555-1011, ext. 12.

Situation Wanted — Dependable Child Care — Will provide child care in my home for infant or toddler. Nutritious meals and TLC. Reasonable rates. Call Debbie 555-4444.

Caretake for Seniors. Young h.s. grad enjoys working w. older citizens. Strong, willing, avail. immed. Have refs. Seeks f/t emp. gd. bnfts. 555-8275. Ask for Sam.

Abbreviations

People who place classified ads often use abbreviated words to make an ad as short as possible. Read the classified ad section in your newspaper to become familiar with abbreviations. Here is a short list to help you now:

excel —— excellent	f.t.
bnfts.—— benefits	or f/t — full time
exp —— experience	emp.—— employment
p.t.	gd. —— good
or p/t — part time	refs.—— references
h.s.—— high school	ext.—— extension
grad—— graduate	req.—— required
w. —— with	sal. —— salary
avail.—— available	

Civil Service   Federal, state, and local governments offer many jobs in community services. Find the civil service office near you and inquire. See the feature on the top of the next page. It explains more about civil service exams.

Unions   Find out about labor unions that may be involved with jobs in the field of community services. Check with union locals in your town; you can find phone numbers in the phone book.

Temporary Employment   Working on a temporary basis can lead to other jobs or to part-time or full-time work. Seasonal work is available for jobs such as refuse worker, child-care or geriatric worker, and teacher's aide.

Applying in Person

Applying to a company in person can be a good idea. Call for an appointment and tell the human resources officer that you would like to have an interview. Some employers may ask that you send a letter or résumé first.

Sending Letters

Writing letters to companies can be an effective way to ask about jobs. Typed letters are preferred, but neat, handwritten letters are acceptable. Check the yellow pages or industry magazines at the public library for companies' addresses. The reference librarian can help you. Address letters to the company's personnel or human resources department. Send your resume with the letter. Keep copies of all letters and follow up in a couple of weeks with another letter.

Résumé

A résumé is a useful one-page outline of information about you that introduces you to a possible future employer. Based on your strengths list, it summarizes your education, work history, and skills.

You will enclose your résumé in letters you write future employers. You also will take it with you to give to your interviewer. Look at the sample résumé on page 87 to see how a typical résumé looks.

Always put your full name, address, and phone number at the top of the résumé. Type the résumé, if possible, or write it by hand neatly. Then state your objective, or the job you are applying for. Put down any experience that shows you are a good worker. Volunteer work and part-time jobs tell an employer that you are always looking to help out and work hard. Put down your most recent job first.

Finally, include information about your education. You can also list any special skills, awards, or honors you have received.

Writing Letters

When you send your résumé in the mail, always attach a cover letter. Your letter will be short, no more than two or three paragraphs. It should come right to the point and lead the employer to your résumé.

Explain what job you are interested in, and include a short listing of your qualifications. Your letter should catch the employer's interest so that the employer wants to turn to your résumé. See the sample on page 88.

Résumé

Robert L. Roan
120 Cedar Street
Mayville, WI 77777
(111) 555-1234

Objective: To work as a security guard.

Experience

1990   Worked temporary security guard job
            during Christmas vacation at Winters
            Department Store.

1989–90   Worked summer security job at Garden
            Spot Resort Bungalows, Glendale.

Training

First aid training from Oakton Hospital.
Bonded and insured, 1989.

Education

1990   Graduated City High School.

References available on request.

November 1, 1991
Martin R. Woodstein
336 Third Street
Piqua, OH 99999

Ms. Velma Wright
Montvale County Court
Route 404
Sunnyside, TN 55555

Dear Ms. Wright:

I am answering your advertisement for a shorthand reporter that appeared in *The Daily Courier* on October 30.

I graduated from Best Business School's shorthand reporting training program in 1989. I take 170 words of dictation a minute. I also have excellent typing skills.

My goal is to be a court reporter in the Montvale County area. I would be happy to come to your office and take a shorthand speed test.

I look forward to hearing from you at your earliest convenience. I am enclosing my resume to give you an idea of my background.

Thank you in advance for your time.

Sincerely,

Martin R. Woodstein

enclosure

Completing the Application Form

You may have to fill out an application form when applying for a job. (See the sample on pages 90 and 91.) This form asks for your education, experience, work history, and possibly other information.

The employer may mail an application form to you ahead of time or you may be asked to fill it in when you come for the interview.

Follow the instructions carefully and print or type information neatly. Neatness tells the employer that you care about work, can organize information, and that you can think clearly.

Have all information with you when you arrive. You may have to fill in salaries for past jobs, your social security number, the dates you worked, and your past supervisors' names, addresses, and phone numbers.

List your most recent jobs first, as you do on your résumé.

However, do not answer any question that you feel invades your privacy. Laws prevent an employer from asking about race, religion, national origin, age, marital status, family situation, property, car, or arrest record. Unless the question applies directly to the job, you do not have to answer it. (See "Know Your Rights.")

The Interview

How you present yourself in a job interview will tell the employer a lot about you. It can be the biggest single factor that helps an employer decide whether to hire you. Knowing how important an interview is, you should prepare yourself to make a good impression.

APPLICATION FOR EMPLOYMENT

(Please print or type your answers)

PERSONAL INFORMATION   Date _____

Name _____ Social Security Number _____ / _____ / _____

Address _____
          Street and Number   City   State   Zip Code

Telephone number (_____) _____ – _____ (_____) _____ – _____
                    day   evening

Job applied for _____ Salary expected $ _____ per _____

How did you learn of this position? _____

Do you want to work _____ Full time or _____ Part time?

Specify preferred days and hours if you answered part time _____

Have you worked for us before? _____ If yes, when? _____

On what date will you be able to start work? _____

Have you ever been convicted of a crime, excluding misdemeanors and summary offenses?

_____ No   _____ Yes

If yes, describe in full _____

Whom should we notify in case of emergency?

Name _____ Relationship _____

Address _____
          Street and number   City   State   Zip Code

Telephone number (_____) _____ – _____ (_____) _____ – _____
                    day   evening

EDUCATION

Type of School	Name and Address	Years Attended	Graduated	Course or Major
High School			Yes No	
College			Yes No	
Post-graduate			Yes No	
Business or Trade			Yes No	
Military or other			Yes No	

WORK EXPERIENCE (List in order, beginning with most recent job)

Dates		Employer's Name and Address	Rate of Pay Start/Finish	Position Held	Reason for Leaving
From	To				

ACTIVITIES AND HONORS (List any academic, extracurricular, civic, or other achievements you consider significant.)

PERSONAL REFERENCES

Name and Occupation	Address	Phone Number

PLEASE READ THE FOLLOWING STATEMENTS CAREFULLY AND SIGN BELOW:

The information that I have provided on this application is accurate to the best of my knowledge and is subject to validation. I authorize the schools, persons, current employer, and other organizations or employers named in this application to provide any relevant information that may be required to arrive at an employment decision.

Applicant's Signature   Date

Before you go to the interview, sit down and prepare what you will say. Think of why you want the job, your experience, and why you qualify. Know as much about the job and the company as possible through ads, brochures, or employees. This will show that you are interested in the company's needs.

Make a list of questions you have. And try to guess what the interviewer will ask. You may ask if you can work overtime or if you can take courses for more training or education. Bring in any certificates or licenses you may need to show.

Dress neatly and appropriately for the interview. Make sure you know exactly where the interview will take place so you will be on time. Allow extra time to get there in case you are delayed by traffic or for some other reason.

Following Up

After the interview, thank the interviewer for his or her time and shake hands. If the job appeals to you, tell the person that you are interested.

When you get back home, send a letter thanking the interviewer for his or her time. Repeat things that were discussed in the interview. Keep a copy of it for yourself and start a file for all future letters.

Think about how you acted in the interview. Did you ask the right questions? Were your answers right? If you feel you should have done something differently, make notes so you can do better the next time.

If you do not hear from the company in two weeks, write a letter to the interviewer repeating your interest. You can also phone to follow up.

Know Your Rights: What Is the Law?

Federal   Under federal law, employers cannot discriminate on the basis of race, religion, sex, national origin, ancestry, or age. People aged forty to seventy are specifically protected against age discrimination. Handicapped workers also are protected. Of course, these laws protect only workers who do their job. Employers are not stopped from hiring workers who are not qualified or firing workers who do not perform.

State   Many states have laws against discrimination based on age, handicap, or membership in armed services reserves. Laws differ from state to state. In some states, there can be no enforced retirement age. And some protect people suffering from AIDS.

Applications   When filling out applications, you do not have to answer questions that may discriminate. Questions about whether you are married, have children, own property or a car, or have an arrest record do not have to be answered. An employer may ask, however, if you have ever been convicted of a crime.

At Work   It is against the law for employers to discriminate against workers when setting hours, workplace conditions, salary, hirings, layoffs, firings, or promotions. And no employer can treat a worker unfairly if he or she has filed a discrimination suit or taken other legal action.

Read Your Contract   Read any work contract you are given. Do not sign it until you understand and agree to everything in it. Ask questions if you have them. If you have used an employment agency, before you sign a contract, settle on whether you pay the fee for finding a job or the employer does.

When Discrimination Occurs: What You Can Do

Government Help   Call the Equal Employment Opportunities Commission or the state Civil Rights Commission if you feel you've been discriminated against. If they think you have been unfairly treated, they may take legal action. If you have been unfairly denied a job, you may get it. If you have been unfairly fired, you may get your job back and receive pay that is owed you. Any mention of the actions taken against you may be removed from your work records. To file a lawsuit, you will need a lawyer.

Private Help   Private organizations like the American Civil Liberties Union (ACLU) and the National Association for the Advancement of Colored People (NAACP) fight against discrimination. They can give you advice.

Sources

General Career Information

Career Information Center, 4th ed., 13 vols. Mission Hills, Cal.: Glencoe/Macmillan, 1990.

Harrington, Thomas, and O'Shea, Arthur (eds.). *Guide for Occupational Exploration.* Circle Pines, Minn.: American Guidance Service, 1984.

Hopke, William E., et al. (eds.). *The Encyclopedia of Career and Vocational Guidance,* 7th ed., 3 vols. Chicago: Ferguson, 1987.

U.S. Government Printing Office. *Occupational Outlook Handbook.* Washington, D.C.: U.S. Government Printing Office, revised biennially.

Community Services

Cornelius, Hal. *Career Guide for Paralegals.* New York: Monarch Press, 1983.

Edelfelt, Roy A. *Careers in Education.* Lincolnwood, Ill.: National Textbook Company, 1988.

Krannich, Ronald L., and Krannich, Caryl Rae. *The Complete Guide to Public Employment.* Masassas, Va.: Impact Publications, 1986.

McDonald, Robert W. *Exploring Careers in the Military Services.* New York: Rosen Publishing Group, 1987.

Murray, Martin. *Your Future Working with Older Adults.* New York: Rosen Press, 1985.

Steinberg, E. P. *You As a Law Enforcement Officer.* New York: Arco, 1985.

Index